Arundhati Roy is the author of *The God of Small Things*
and *The End of Imagination*.

THE
GREATER
COMMON
GOOD

The Author's Royalties have been assigned to the
NARMADA BACHAO ANDOLAN

IndiaBook Distributors (Bombay) Ltd.
1007/1008, Arcadia, 195 Nariman Point,
Bombay 400 020.

This first Indian edition published by India Book Distributers
(Bombay) Ltd. 1999

1 3 5 7 9 10 8 6 4 2

ISBN 81-7310-121-3

Design: Tara Sahgal

Set in Monotype Baskerville
Printed and bound by Thomson Press, India

Photo Credits
Cover & pages 35, 46, 59, 60 - Anurag Singh; page 37 - NBA;
pages 1, 16 - Sanjiv Bamroo/Sanctuary; pages 41, 47 - Farhatullah Beig
page 5 - The Hindu Photo library
Author's Photo: Jo Selsing

For

The Narmada, and all the life she sustains

And

Shripad, Nandini, Sylvie, Alok, Medha, Baba Amte and their colleagues in the NBA

Extraordinary people fighting an extraordinary war

ACKNOWLEDGEMENTS

There are two men who fall into the *"without whom"* (this book couldn't have been written) category:

Himanshu Thakker, who first revealed to me - brilliantly, meticulously, almost shyly - the horrors of the Narmada Valley Development Projects. To him I owe my first (belated) conspectus of this intricate method of pulverising a people.

Patrick McCully, who I've never met, but whose book *Silenced Rivers* is the rock on which this work stands. If you want to read a truly dazzling book on Big Dams, drop mine and read his.

Jharana Jhaveri, most tenacious of fighters and gentlest of friends, thank you for travelling with me. All the way.

Deepak Sarkar and Anurag Singh, for your friendship and cool, organized wisdom and advice.

Tara and Bittu Sahgal for their help and support.

N.Ram and Vinod Mehta, editors of OUTLOOK and FRONTLINE, who first published *The Greater Common Good*. It's reassuring to know that big men still take big risks. There aren't many like you around.

Jojo Van Gruisen, Golak Khandual, Arjun Raina, Sanjay Kak. Old Soul friends. Fellow travellers on this path.

Finally, Pradip Krishen without whom my life would not be fully lived.

Thankyou.

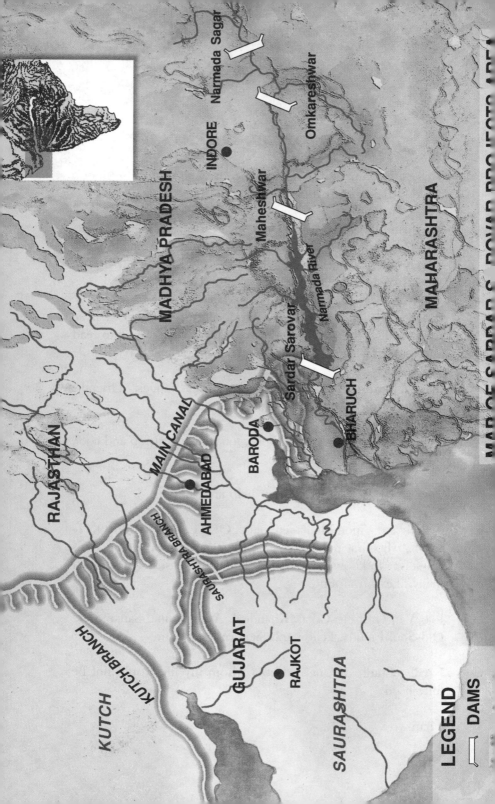

MAP OF SARDAR SAROVAR PROJECTS (SSP)

LEGEND
⊏ DAMS

Narmada Sagar

Omkareshwar

INDORE

Maheshwar

MADHYA PRADESH

Narmada River

Sardar Sarovar

MAHARASHTRA

BHARUCH

BARODA

MAIN CANAL

RAJASTHAN

AHMEDABAD

SAURASHTRA BRANCH

KUTCH BRANCH

KUTCH

GUJARAT

RAJKOT

SAURASHTRA

"If you are to suffer, you should suffer in the interest of the country..."

Jawaharlal Nehru, speaking to villagers who were to be displaced by the Hirakud dam, 1948[1]

I stood on a hill and laughed out loud.

I had crossed the Narmada by boat from Jalsindhi and climbed the headland on the opposite bank from where I could see, ranged across the crowns of low, bald hills, the tribal hamlets of Sikka, Surung, Neemgavan and Domkhedi. I could see their airy, fragile homes. I could see their fields and the forests behind them. I could see little children with littler goats scuttling across the landscape like motorized peanuts. I knew I was looking at a civilisation older than Hinduism, slated - *sanctioned* (by the highest court in the land) - to be drowned this monsoon when the waters of the Sardar Sarovar reservoir will rise to submerge it.

1

Why did I laugh?

Because I suddenly remembered the tender concern with which the Supreme Court judges in Delhi (before vacating the legal stay on further construction of the Sardar Sarovar dam) had enquired whether tribal children in the resettlement colonies would have children's parks to play in. The lawyers representing the Government had hastened to assure them that indeed they would, and what's more, that there were seesaws and slides and swings in every park. I looked up at the endless sky and down at the river rushing past and for a brief, brief moment the absurdity of it all reversed my rage and I laughed. I meant no disrespect.

Let me say at the outset that I'm not a city-basher. I've done my time in a village. I've had first hand experience of the isolation, the inequity and the potential savagery of it. I'm not an anti-development junkie, nor a proselytiser for the eternal upholding of custom and tradition. What I *am,* however, is curious. Curiosity took me to the Narmada valley. Instinct told me that this was the big one. The one in which the battle-lines were clearly drawn, the warring armies massed along them. The one in which it would be possible to wade through the congealed morass of hope, anger, information, disinformation, political artifice, engineering ambition, disingenuous socialism, radical activism, bureaucratic subterfuge, misinformed emotionalism and of course the pervasive, invariably dubious, politics of International Aid.

Instinct led me to set aside Joyce and Nabokov, to postpone reading Don DeLillo's big book and substitute it with reports on drainage and irrigation, with journals and books and documentary films about dams and why they're built and what they do.
My first tentative questions revealed that few people know what is really going on in the Narmada valley. Those who know, know

2

a lot. Most know nothing at all. And yet, almost everyone has a passionate opinion. Nobody's neutral. I realised very quickly that I was straying into mined territory.

In India over the last ten years the fight against the Sardar Sarovar dam has come to represent far more than the fight for one river. This has been its strength as well its weakness. Some years ago, it became a debate that captured the popular imagination. That's what raised the stakes and changed the complexion of the battle. From being a fight over the fate of a river valley it began to raise doubts about an entire political system. What is at issue now is the very nature of our democracy. Who owns this land? Who owns its rivers? Its forests? Its fish? These are huge questions. They are being taken hugely seriously by the State. They are being answered in one voice by every institution at its command - the army, the police, the bureaucracy, the courts. And not just answered, but answered unambiguously, in bitter, brutal ways.

For the people of the valley, the fact that the stakes were raised to this degree has meant that their most effective weapon - *specific* facts about *specific* issues in this *specific* valley - has been blunted by the debate on the big issues. The basic premise of the argument has been inflated until it has burst into bits that have, over time, bobbed away. Occasionally a disconnected piece of the puzzle floats by - an emotionally charged account of the Government's callous treatment of displaced people; an outburst at how the Narmada Bachao Andolan (NBA), 'a handful of activists', is holding the nation to ransom; a legal correspondent reporting on the progress of the NBA's writ petition in the Supreme Court.

Though there has been a fair amount of writing on the subject, most of it is for a 'special interest' readership. News reports tend to be about isolated aspects of the project. Government documents are classified as 'Secret'. I think it's fair to say that public perception of the issue is pretty crude and is divided crudely, into two categories:

On the one hand, it is seen as a war between modern, rational, progressive forces of 'Development' Vs a sort of neo-Luddite impulse - an irrational, emotional 'Anti-Development' resistance, fuelled by an arcadian, pre-industrial dream.

On the other, as a Nehru Vs Gandhi contest. This lifts the whole sorry business out of the bog of deceit, lies, false promises and increasingly successful propaganda (which is what it's *really* about) and confers on it a false legitimacy. It makes out that both sides have the Greater Good of the Nation in mind - but merely disagree about the means by which to achieve it.

Both interpretations put a tired spin on the dispute. Both stir up emotions that cloud the particular facts of this particular story. Both are indications of how urgently we need new heroes - new *kinds* of heroes - and how we've overused our old ones (like we overbowl our bowlers).

The Nehru Vs Gandhi argument pushes this very contemporary issue back into an old bottle. Nehru and Gandhi were generous men. Their paradigms for development are based on assumptions of inherent morality. Nehru's on the paternal, protective morality of the Soviet-style centralised State. Gandhi's on the nurturing, maternal morality of romanticised village Republics. Both would probably work, if only we were better human beings. If we all wore khadi and suppressed our base urges. Fifty years down the line, it's safe to say that we haven't made the grade. We haven't even come close. We need an up-dated insurance plan against our own basic natures.
It's possible that as a nation we've exhausted our quota of heroes for this century, but while we wait for shiny new ones to come along, we have to limit the damage. We have to support our

small heroes. (Of these we have many. Many.) We have to fight specific wars in specific ways. Who knows, perhaps that's what the twenty-first century has in store for us. The dismantling of the Big. Big bombs, big dams, big ideologies, big contradictions, big countries, big wars, big heroes, big mistakes. Perhaps it will be the Century of the Small. Perhaps right now, this very minute, there's a small god up in heaven readying herself for us. Could it be? Could it *possibly* be? It sounds finger-licking good to me.

I was drawn to the valley because I sensed that the fight for the Narmada had entered a newer, sadder phase. I went because writers are drawn to stories the way vultures are drawn to kills. My motive was not compassion. It was sheer greed. I was right. I found a story there.

And what a story it is...

Homes at Manibeli submerged by the Sardar Sarovar reservoir during the monsoon of 1993.

"People say that the Sardar Sarovar dam is an expensive project. But it is bringing drinking water to millions. This is our lifeline. Can you put a price on this? Does the air we breathe have a price? We will live. We will drink. We will bring glory to the state of Gujarat."

> \- Urmilaben Patel, wife of Gujarat Chief Minister Chimanbhai Patel, speaking at a public rally in Delhi in 1993.

"We will request you to move from your houses after the dam comes up. If you move it will be good. Otherwise we shall release the waters and drown you all."

> \- Morarji Desai, speaking at a public meeting in the submergence zone of the Pong dam in 1961.[2]

"Why didn't they just poison us? Then we wouldn't have to live in this shit-hole and the Government could have survived alone with its precious dam all to itself."

> \- Ram Bai, whose village was submerged when the Bargi dam was built on the Narmada. She now lives in a slum in Jabalpur.[3]

In the fifty years since Independence, after Nehru's famous "Dams are the Temples of Modern India" speech, (one that he grew to regret in his own lifetime[4]) his footsoldiers threw themselves into the business of building dams with unnatural fervour. Dam-building grew to be equated with Nation-building. Their enthusiasm alone should have been reason enough to make one suspicious. Not only did they build new dams and new irrigation systems, they took control of small, traditional systems that had been managed by village communities for thousands of years, and allowed them to atrophy.[5] To compensate the loss, the Government built more and more dams. Big ones, little ones, tall ones, short ones. The result of its exertions is that India now boasts of being the world's third largest dam builder. According to the Central Water Commission, we have three thousand six hundred dams that qualify as Big Dams, three thousand three hundred of them built after Independence. One thousand more are under construction.[6] Yet one fifth of our population - 200 million people - does not have safe drinking water and two-thirds - 600 million - lack basic sanitation.[7]

Big Dams started well, but have ended badly. There was a time when everybody loved them, everybody had them - the Communists, Capitalists, Christians, Muslims, Hindus, Buddhists. There was a time when Big Dams moved men to poetry. Not any longer. All over the world there is a movement growing against Big Dams.
In the First World they're being de-commissioned, blown up.[8] The fact that they do more harm than good is no longer just conjecture. Big Dams are obsolete. They're uncool. They're undemocratic. They're a Government's way of accumulating authority (deciding who will get how much water and who will grow what where). They're a guaranteed way of taking a farmer's wisdom away from him. They're a brazen means of taking water, land and irrigation away from the poor and gifting it to the rich.

7

Their reservoirs displace huge populations of people leaving them homeless and destitute.

Ecologically too, they're in the doghouse.[9] They lay the earth to waste. They cause floods, water-logging, salinity, they spread disease. There is mounting evidence that links Big Dams to earthquakes.

Big Dams haven't really lived up to their role as the monuments of Modern Civilisation, emblems of Man's ascendancy over Nature. Monuments are supposed to be timeless, but dams have an all too finite lifetime. They last only as long as it takes Nature to fill them with silt.[10] It's common knowledge now that Big Dams do the opposite of what their Publicity People say they do - the Local Pain for National Gain myth has been blown wide open.

For all these reasons, the dam-building industry in the First World is in trouble and out of work. So it's exported to the Third World in the name of Development Aid,[11] along with their other waste like old weapons, superannuated aircraft carriers and banned pesticides.

On the one hand the Indian Government, *every* Indian Government, rails self-righteously against the First World, and on the other, actually *pays* to receive their gift-wrapped garbage. Aid is just another praetorian business enterprise. Like Colonialism was. It has destroyed most of Africa. Bangladesh is reeling from its ministrations. We *know* all this, in numbing detail. Yet in India our leaders welcome it with slavish smiles (and make nuclear bombs to shore up their flagging self-esteem).

Over the last fifty years India has spent Rs 87,000 crores[12] on the irrigation sector alone.[13] Yet there are more drought-prone areas and more flood-prone areas today than there were in 1947.[14] Despite the disturbing evidence of irrigation disasters, dam-induced floods and rapid disenchantment with the Green

Revolution[15] (declining yields, degraded land), the government has not commissioned a post-project evaluation of a *single one* of its 3,600 dams to gauge whether or not it has achieved what it set out to achieve, whether or not the (always phenomenal) costs were justified, or even what the costs actually were.

The Government of India has detailed figures for how many million tonnes of food grain or edible oils the country produces and how much more we produce now than we did in 1947. It can tell you how much bauxite is mined in a year or what the total surface area of the National Highways adds up to. It's possible to access minute to minute information about the stock exchange or the value of the rupee in the world market. We know how many cricket matches we've lost on a Friday in Sharjah. It's not hard to find out how many graduates India produces, or how many men had vasectomies in any given year. But the Government of India does not have a figure for the number of people that have been displaced by dams or sacrificed in other ways at the altars of 'National Progress.' Isn't this *astounding?* How can you measure Progress if you don't know what it costs and who has paid for it? How can the 'market' put a price on things - food, clothes, electricity, running water - when it doesn't take into account the *real* cost of production?

According to a detailed study of 54 Large Dams done by the Indian Institute of Public Administration,[16] the *average* number of people displaced by a Large Dam in India is 44,182. Admittedly, 54 dams out of 3,300 is not a big enough sample. But since it's all we have, let's try and do some rough arithmetic. A first draft.

To err on the side of caution, let's halve the number of people. Or, let's err on the side of *abundant* caution and take an average of just 10,000 people per Large Dam. It's an improbably low figure, I know, but... never mind. Whip out your calculators.

9

$$3,300 \times 10,000 = 33,000,000$$

That's what it works out to. 33 *million* people. Displaced by Big Dams *alone* in the last fifty years. What about those that have been displaced by the thousands of other Development Projects? At a private lecture, N.C. Saxena, Secretary to the Planning Commission, said he thought the number was in the region of 50 million (of which 40 million were displaced by dams).[17] We daren't say so, because it isn't official. It isn't official because we daren't say so. You have to murmur it for fear of being accused of hyperbole. You have to whisper it to yourself, because it really does sound unbelievable. It *can't be*, I've been telling myself. I must have got the zeroes muddled. *It can't be true*. I barely have the courage to say it aloud. To run the risk of sounding like a 'sixties hippie dropping acid ("It's the System, man!"), or a paranoid schizophrenic with a persecution complex. But it *is* the System, man. What else can it be?

50 million people.

Go on, Government, quibble. Bargain. Beat it down. Say *something.*

I feel like someone who's just stumbled on a mass grave.

Fifty million is more than the population of Gujarat. Almost three times the population of Australia. More than three times the number of refugees that Partition created in India. Ten times the number of Palestinian refugees. The western world today is convulsed over the future of one million people who have fled from Kosovo.

A huge percentage of the displaced are tribal people (57.6% in the case of the Sardar Sarovar dam).[18] Include Dalits and the figure becomes obscene. According to the Commissioner for

10

Scheduled Castes and Tribes it's about 60%.[19] If you consider that tribal people account for only 8%, and Dalits another 15%, of India's population, it opens up a whole other dimension to the story. The ethnic 'otherness' of their victims takes some of the pressure off the Nation Builders. It's like having an expense account. Someone else pays the bills. People from another country. Another world. India's poorest people are subsidising the lifestyles of her richest.

Did I hear someone say something about the world's biggest democracy?

What has happened to all these millions of people? Where are they now? How do they earn a living? Nobody really knows. (Recently, the Indian Express had an account of how tribal people displaced from the Nagarjunasagar dam Project are selling their babies to foreign adoption agencies.[20] The Government intervened and put the babies in two public hospitals where 6 infants died of neglect.) When it comes to Rehabilitation, the Government's priorities are clear. India does not *have* a National Rehabilitation Policy. According to the Land Acquisition Act of 1894 (amended in 1984) the Government is not legally bound to provide a displaced person anything but a cash compensation. Imagine that. A cash compensation, to be paid by an Indian government official to an illiterate tribal man (the women get nothing) in a land where even the postman demands a tip for a delivery! Most tribal people have no formal title to their land and therefore cannot claim compensation anyway. Most tribal people - or let's say most small farmers - have as much use for money as a Supreme Court judge has for a bag of fertiliser.

The millions of displaced people don't exist anymore. When history is written they won't be in it. Not even as statistics. Some of them have subsequently been displaced three and four times - a dam, an artillery proof range, another dam, a uranium

11

mine, a power project. Once they start rolling there's no resting place. The great majority is eventually absorbed into slums on the periphery of our great cities, where it coalesces into an immense pool of cheap construction labour (that builds more projects that displace more people). True, they're not being annihilated or taken to gas chambers, but I can warrant that the quality of their accommodation is worse than in any concentration camp of the Third Reich. They're not captive, but they redefine the meaning of liberty.

And still the nightmare doesn't end. They continue to be uprooted even from their hellish hovels by government bulldozers that fan out on clean-up missions whenever elections are comfortingly far away and the urban rich get twitchy about hygiene. In cities like Delhi, they run the risk of being shot by the police for shitting in public places - like three slum-dwellers were, not more than two years ago.

In the French Canadian wars of the 1770s, Lord Amherst exterminated most of Canada's Native Indians by offering them blankets infested with the smallpox virus. Two centuries on, we of the Real India have found less obvious ways of achieving similar ends.

The millions of displaced people in India are nothing but refugees of an unacknowledged war. And we, like the citizens of White America and French Canada and Hitler's Germany, are condoning it by looking away. Why? Because we're told that it's being done for the sake of the Greater Common Good. That it's being done in the name of Progress, in the name of the National Interest (which, of course, is paramount). Therefore gladly, unquestioningly, almost gratefully, we believe what we're told. We believe that it benefits us to believe.

Allow me to shake your faith. Put your hand in mine and let me lead you through the maze. Do this, because it's important that you understand. If you find reason to disagree, by all means take the other side. But please don't ignore it, don't look away. It isn't an easy tale to tell. It's full of numbers and explanations. Numbers used to make my eyes glaze over. Not any more. Not since I began to follow the direction in which they point.

Trust me. There's a story here.

It's true that India has progressed. It's true that in 1947, when Colonialism formally ended, India was food deficit. In 1950 we produced 51 million tonnes of food grain. Today we produce close to 200 million tonnes.[21]
It's true that in 1995 the state granaries were overflowing with 30 million tonnes of unsold grain. It's also true that at the same time, forty percent of India's population - more than 350 million people - were living below the poverty line.[22] That's more than the country's population in 1947.

Indians are too poor to buy the food their country produces. Indians are being forced to grow the kinds of food they can't afford to eat themselves. Look at what happened in Kalahandi District in Western Orissa, best known for its starvation deaths. In the drought of 1996, people died of starvation (16 according to the State, over a 100 according to the press).[23] Yet that same year rice production in Kalahandi was higher than the national average! Rice was exported from Kalahandi District to the Centre.

Certainly India has progressed but most of its people haven't. Our leaders say that we must have nuclear missiles to protect us from the threat of China and Pakistan. But who will protect us from ourselves?

What kind of country is this? Who owns it? Who runs it? What's going on?
It's time to spill a few State Secrets. To puncture the myth about

13

the inefficient, bumbling, corrupt, but ultimately genial, essentially democratic, Indian State. Carelessness cannot account for fifty million disappeared people. Nor can Karma. Let's not delude ourselves. There is method here, precise, relentless and one hundred percent man-made.

The Indian State is not a State that has failed. It is a State that has succeeded impressively in what it set out to do. It has been ruthlessly efficient in the way it has appropriated India's resources - its land, its water, its forests, its fish, its meat, its eggs, its air - and redistributed it to a favoured few (in return, no doubt, for a few favours). It is superbly accomplished in the art of protecting its cadres of paid-up elite, consummate in its methods of pulverising those who inconvenience its intentions. But its finest feat of all is the way it achieves all this and emerges smelling sweet. The way it manages to keep its secrets, to contain information - that vitally concerns the daily lives of one billion people - in government files, accessible only to the keepers of the flame: ministers, bureaucrats, state engineers, defence strategists. Of course we make it easy for them, we, its beneficiaries. We take care not to dig too deep. We don't really *want* to know the grisly detail.

Thanks to us, Independence came (and went), elections come and go, but there has been no shuffling of the deck. On the contrary, the old order has been consecrated, the rift fortified. We, the Rulers, won't pause to look up from our heaving table. We don't seem to know that the resources we're feasting on, are finite and rapidly depleting. There's cash in the bank, but soon there'll be nothing left to buy with it. The food's running out in the kitchen. And the servants haven't eaten yet. Actually, the servants stopped eating a long time ago.

India lives in her villages, we're told, in every other sanctimonious public speech. That's bullshit. It's just another fig leaf from the

14

Government's bulging wardrobe. India doesn't live in her villages. India *dies* in her villages. India gets kicked around in her villages. India lives in her cities. India's villages live only to serve her cities. Her villagers are her citizens' vassals and for that reason must be controlled and kept alive, but only just.

This impression we have of an overstretched State, struggling to cope with the sheer weight and scale of its problems, is a dangerous one. The fact is that it's *creating* the problem. It's a giant poverty-producing machine, masterful in its methods of pitting the poor against the very poor, of flinging crumbs to the wretched so that they dissipate their energies fighting each other, while peace (and advertising) reigns in the Master's Lodgings.

Until this process is recognised for what it is, until it is addressed and attacked, elections - however fiercely they're contested - will continue to be mock battles that serve only to further entrench unspeakable inequity. Democracy (our version of it) will continue to be the benevolent mask behind which a pestilence flourishes unchallenged. On a scale that will make old wars and past misfortunes look like controlled laboratory experiments. Already fifty million people have been fed into the Development Mill and have emerged as airconditioners and popcorn and rayon suits - *subsidised* airconditioners and popcorn and rayon suits. If we must have these nice things - and they *are* nice - at least we should be made to pay for them.

There's a hole in the flag that needs mending.

It's a sad thing to have to say, but as long as we have faith - we have no hope. To hope, we have to *break* the faith. We have to fight specific wars in specific ways and we have to fight to win. Listen then, to the story of the Narmada Valley. Understand it. And, if you wish, enlist. Who knows, it may lead to magic.

15

The Narmada wells up on the plateau of Amarkantak in the Shahdol district of Madhya Pradesh, then winds its way through 1,300 kilometres of beautiful broadleaved forest and perhaps the most fertile agricultural land in India. Twenty five million people live in the river valley, linked to the ecosystem and to each other by an ancient, intricate web of interdependence (and, no doubt, exploitation).

Though the Narmada has been targeted for "water resource development" for more than fifty years now, the reason it has, until recently, evaded being captured and dismembered is that it flows through three states - Madhya Pradesh, Maharashtra and Gujarat.

Ninety per cent of the river flows through Madhya Pradesh; it merely skirts the northern border of Maharashtra, then flows through Gujarat for about 180 kilometres before emptying into the Arabian sea at Bharuch.

As early as 1946, plans had been afoot to dam the river at Gora in Gujarat. In 1961, Nehru laid the foundation stone for a 49.8 metre high dam - the midget progenitor of the Sardar Sarovar.

Around the same time, the Survey of India drew up new topographical maps of the river basin. The dam planners in Gujarat studied the new maps and decided that it would be more profitable to build a much bigger dam. But this meant hammering out an agreement with neighbouring states.

For years the three states bickered and balked but failed to agree on a water-sharing formula. Eventually, in 1969, the Central Government set up the Narmada Water Disputes Tribunal. It took the Tribunal another ten years to announce its Award. *The people whose lives were going to be devastated were neither informed nor consulted nor heard.*

To apportion shares in the waters, the first, most basic thing the Tribunal had to do was to find out how much water there was in the river. Usually this can only be reliably estimated if there is at least forty years of recorded data on the volume of actual flow in the river. Since this was not available, they decided to extrapolate from rainfall data. They arrived at a figure of 27.22 million acre feet (MAF).[24]

This figure is the statistical bedrock of the Narmada Valley Projects. We are still living with its legacy. It more or less determines the overall design of the Projects - the height, location and number of dams. By inference, it determines the cost of the Projects, how much area will be submerged, how many people will be displaced and what the benefits will be.

In 1992, actual observed flow data for the Narmada - which was now available for 45 years (from 1948 to1992) - showed that the yield from the river was only 22.69 MAF - eighteen percent less![25] The Central Water Commission admits that there is less water in the Narmada than had previously been assumed[26]. The Government of India says:

17

> *It may be noted that clause II* (of the Decision of
> the Tribunal) *relating to determination of*
> *dependable flow as 28 MAF is non-reviewable* (!)[27]

Never mind the data - the Narmada is legally bound by human
decree to produce as much water as the Government of India
commands.

Its proponents boast that the Narmada Valley Project is the most
ambitious river valley project ever conceived in human history.
They plan to build 3,200 dams that will reconstitute the Narmada
and her 41 tributaries into a series of step reservoirs - an immense
staircase of amenable water. Of these, 30 will be major dams,
135 medium and the rest small. Two of the major dams will be
multipurpose mega dams. The Sardar Sarovar in Gujarat and
the Narmada Sagar in Madhya Pradesh will, between them, hold
more water than any other reservoir on the Indian subcontinent.

Whichever way you look at it, the Narmada Valley Development
Project is Big. It will alter the ecology of the entire river basin of
one of India's biggest rivers. For better or for worse, it will affect
the lives of twenty five million people who live in the valley. It
will submerge and destroy 4,000 square kilometres of natural
deciduous forest.[28] Yet, even before the Ministry of
Environment cleared the project, the World Bank offered to
finance the lynchpin of the project - the Sardar Sarovar dam,
whose reservoir displaces people in Madhya Pradesh and
Maharashtra, but whose benefits go to Gujarat. The Bank was
ready with its cheque-book *before* any costs were computed,
before any studies had been done, *before* anybody had any
idea of what the human cost or the environmental impact of
the dam would be!

The 450 million dollar loan for the Sardar Sarovar Projects was
sanctioned and in place in 1985. The Ministry of Environment

clearance for the project came only in 1987! Talk about enthusiasm. It fairly borders on evangelism. Can anybody care so much?

Why were they so keen?

Between 1947 and 1994 the World Bank received 6,000 applications for loans from around the world. It didn't turn down a single one. *Not a single one.* Terms like 'Moving money' and 'Meeting loan targets' suddenly begin to make sense.

India is in a situation today where it pays back more money to The Bank in interest and repayment instalments than it receives from it. We are forced to incur new debts in order to be able to repay our old ones. According to the World Bank Annual Report, last year (1998), after the arithmetic, India paid The Bank $478 million more than it borrowed. Over the last five years (1993 to 1998) India paid The Bank $1.475 billion more than it received.[29]
The relationship between us is exactly like the relationship between a landless labourer steeped in debt and the local Bania - it is an affectionate relationship, the poor man loves his Bania because he's always there when he's needed. It's not for nothing that we call the world a Global Village. The only difference between the landless labourer and the Government of India is that one uses the money to survive. The other just funnels it into the private coffers of its officers and agents, pushing the country into an economic bondage that it may never overcome.

The international Dam Industry is worth $20 billion a year.[30] If you follow the trails of Big Dams the world over, wherever you go - China, Japan, Malaysia, Thailand, Brazil, Guatemala - you'll rub up against the same story, encounter the same actors: the Iron Triangle (dam-jargon for the nexus between politicians, bureaucrats and dam construction companies), the racketeers

19

who call themselves International Environmental Consultants (who are usually directly employed by dam-builders or their subsidiaries), and more often than not, the friendly neighbourhood World Bank. You'll grow to recognise the same inflated rhetoric, the same noble 'Peoples' Dam' slogans, the same swift, brutal repression that follows the first sign of civil insubordination. (Of late, especially after its experience in the Narmada Valley, The Bank is more cautious about choosing the countries in which it finances projects that involve mass displacement. At present, China is its Most Favoured client. It's the great irony of our times - American citizens protest the massacre in Tiananmen square, but The Bank has used their money to fund studies for the Three Gorges dam in China which is going to displace 1.3 million people. The Bank is today the biggest foreign financier of large dams in China. [31]

It's a skilful circus and the acrobats know each other well. Occasionally they'll swap parts - a bureaucrat will join The Bank, a Banker will surface as a Project Consultant. At the end of play, a huge percentage of what's called 'Development Aid' is re-channelled back to the countries it came from, masquerading as equipment cost or consultants' fees or salaries to the agencies' own staff. Often Aid is openly 'tied' (as in the case of the Japanese loan for the Sardar Sarovar dam - tied to a contract for purchasing turbines from the Sumitomo Corporation.)[32] Sometimes the connections are more sleazy. In 1993, Britain financed the Pergau Dam in Malaysia with a subsidised loan of 234 million pounds, despite an Overseas Development Administration report that said that the dam would be a 'bad buy' for Malaysia. It later emerged that the loan was offered to 'encourage' Malaysia to sign a 1.3 *billion* pound contract to buy British Arms.[33]

In 1994, British consultants earned $2.5 billion on overseas contracts.[34] The second biggest sector of the market after Project Management was writing what are called EIAs (Environmental

20

Impact Assessments). In the Development racket, the rules are pretty simple. If you get invited by a Government to write an EIA for a big dam project and you point out a problem (say, you quibble about the amount of water available in a river, or, God forbid, you suggest that the human costs are perhaps too high) then you're history. You're an OOWC. An Out Of Work Consultant. And Oops! There goes your Range Rover. There goes your holiday in Tuscany. There goes your children's private boarding school. There's good money in poverty. Plus Perks.

In keeping with Big Dam tradition, concurrent with the construction of the 138.68 metre high Sardar Sarovar dam, began the elaborate Government pantomime of conducting studies to estimate the actual project costs and the impact it would have on people and the environment. The World Bank participated whole-heartedly in the charade - occasionally it beetled its brows and raised feeble requests for more information on issues like the resettlement and rehabilitation of what it calls PAPs - Project Affected Persons. (They help, these acronyms, they manage to mutate muscle and blood into cold statistics. PAPs soon cease to be people.)
The merest crumbs of information satisfied The Bank and it proceeded with the project. The implicit, unwritten but fairly obvious understanding between the concerned agencies was that whatever the costs - economic, environmental or human - the project would go ahead. They would justify it as they went along. They knew full well that eventually, in a courtroom or to a committee, no argument works as well as a Fait Accompli.
Mi' lord, the country is losing two crores a day due to the delay.

The Government refers to the Sardar Sarovar Projects as the 'Most Studied Project in India', yet the game goes something like this: when the Tribunal first announced its Award and the Gujarat Government announced its plan of how it was going to use its share of water, *there was no mention of drinking water*

21

for villages in Kutch and Saurashtra, the arid areas of Gujarat. When the project ran into political trouble, the Government suddenly discovered the emotive power of Thirst. Suddenly, quenching the thirst of parched throats in Kutch and Saurashtra became the whole *point* of the Sardar Sarovar Projects. (Never mind that water from two rivers - the Sabarmati and the Mahi, both of which are *miles* closer to Kutch and Saurashtra than the Narmada, have been dammed and diverted to Ahmedabad, Mehsana and Kheda. Neither Kutch nor Saurashtra have seen a drop of it.) Officially, the number of people who will be provided drinking water by the Sardar Sarovar Canal fluctuates from 28 million (1983) to 32.5 million (1989) - nice touch, the decimal point! - to 40 million (1992) and down to 25 million (1993).[35]

The number of villages that would receive drinking water was zero in 1979, 4,719 in the early '80s, 7,234 in 1990 and 8,215 in 1991.[36] When pressed, the Government admitted that the figures for 1991 included 236 *uninhabited* villages![37]

Every aspect of the project is approached in this almost playful manner, as if it's a family board game. Even when it concerns the lives and futures of vast numbers of people.

In 1979 the number of families that would be displaced by the Sardar Sarovar reservoir was estimated to be a little over 6,000. In 1987 it grew to 12,000. In 1991 it surged to 27,000. In 1992 the Government acknowledged that 40,000 families would be affected. Today, the official figure hovers between 40,000 and 41,500.[38] (Of course even this is an absurd figure, because the reservoir isn't the *only* thing that displaces people. According to the NBA the actual figure is about 85,000 families - that's *half a million* people.)

The estimated cost of the project bounced up from under Rs. 5,000 crores[39] to Rs. 20,000 crores (officially). The NBA says

22

that it will cost Rs. 44,000 crores.[40]

The Government claims the Sardar Sarovar Projects will produce 1,450 megawatts of power.[41] The thing about multi-purpose dams like the Sardar Sarovar is that their 'purposes' (irrigation, power production and flood-control) conflict with each other. Irrigation uses up the water you need to produce power. Flood control requires you to keep the reservoir empty during the monsoon months to deal with an anticipated surfeit of water. And if there's no surfeit, you're left with an empty dam. And this defeats the purpose of irrigation, which is to *store* the monsoon water. It's like the conundrum of trying to ford a river with a fox, a chicken and a bag of grain. The result of these mutually conflicting aims, studies say, is that when the Sardar Sarovar Projects are completed and the scheme is fully functional, it will end up producing only 3% of the power that its planners say it will. About 50 megawatts. And if you take into account the power needed to pump water through its vast network of canals, the Sardar Sarovar Projects will end up *consuming* more electricity than they produce![42]

In an old war, everybody has an axe to grind. So how do you pick your way through these claims and counter-claims? How do you decide whose estimate is more reliable? One way is to take a look at the track record of Indian dams.

The Bargi dam near Jabalpur was the first dam on the Narmada to be completed (in 1990). It cost ten times more than was budgeted and submerged three times more land than the engineers said it would. About 70,000 people from 101 villages were supposed to be displaced, but when they filled the reservoir (without warning anybody), 162 villages were submerged. Some of the resettlement sites built by the Government were submerged as well. People were flushed out like rats from the land they had lived on for centuries. They salvaged what they could, and watched their houses being washed away. 114,000 people were displaced.[43] There was no rehabilitation policy. Some were given meagre cash compensations. Many got absolutely nothing. A few were moved to government rehabilitation sites. The site at Gorakhpur is, according to Government publicity, an 'ideal village'. Between 1990 and 1992, five people died of starvation there. The rest either returned to live illegally in the forests near the reservoir, or moved to slums in Jabalpur.

The Bargi dam irrigates only as much land as it submerged in the first place - *and only 5% of the area that its planners claimed it would irrigate.*[44] Even that is water-logged.

Time and again, it's the same story. The Andhra Pradesh Irrigation II scheme claimed it would displace 63,000 people. When completed, it displaced 150,000 people[45]. The Gujarat Medium Irrigation II scheme displaced 140,000 people instead of 63,600.[46] The revised estimate of the number of people to be displaced by the Upper Krishna irrigation project in Karnataka is 240,000 against its initial claims of displacing only 20,000.[47]

These are World Bank figures. Not the NBA's. Imagine what this does to our conservative estimate of 33 million.

Construction work on the Sardar Sarovar dam site, which had continued sporadically since 1961, began in earnest in 1988. At the time, nobody, not the Government, nor the World Bank, were aware that a woman called Medha Patkar had been wandering through the villages slated to be submerged, asking people whether they had any idea of the plans that the Government had in store for them. When she arrived in the valley all those years ago, opposing the construction of the dam was the furthest thing from her mind. Her chief concern was that displaced villagers should be resettled in an equitable, humane way. It gradually became clear to her that the

24

Government's intentions towards them were far from honourable. By 1986 word had spread and each state had a peoples' organisation that questioned the promises about resettlement and rehabilitation that were being bandied about by Government officials. It was only some years later that the full extent of the horror - the impact that the dams would have, both on the people who were to be displaced and the people who were supposed to benefit - began to surface. The Narmada Valley Development Project came to be known as India's Greatest Planned Environmental Disaster. The various peoples' organisations massed into a single organisation and the Narmada Bachao Andolan - the extraordinary NBA - was born.

In 1988 the NBA formally called for all work on the Narmada Valley Development Projects to be stopped. People declared that they would drown if they had to, but would not move from their homes. Within two years, the struggle had burgeoned and had support from other resistance movements. In September 1989, 50,000 people gathered in the Valley from all over India to pledge to fight Destructive Development. The dam site and its adjacent areas, already under the Indian Official Secrets Act, was clamped under Section 144 which prohibits the gathering of groups of more than five people. The whole area was turned into a police camp. Despite the barricades, one year later, on 28th September 1990, thousands of villagers made their way on foot and by boat to a little town called Badwani, in Madhya Pradesh, to reiterate their pledge to drown rather than agree to move from their homes.

News of the peoples' opposition to the Projects spread to other countries. The Japanese arm of Friends of the Earth mounted a campaign in Japan that succeeded in getting the Government of Japan to withdraw its 27 billion yen loan to finance the Sardar Sarovar Projects. (The contract for the turbines still holds). Once the Japanese withdrew, international pressure from various environmental activist groups who supported the struggle, began to mount on the World Bank.

This of course, led to an escalation of repression in the valley. Government policy, described by a particularly articulate minister, was to "flood the valley with khakhi".

On Christmas Day in 1990, six thousand men and women walked over a hundred kilometres, carrying their provisions and their bedding, accompanying a seven member sacrificial squad that had resolved to lay down its lives for the river. They were stopped at Ferkuwa on the Gujarat border by battalions of armed police and crowds of people from the city of Baroda, many of whom were hired, some of whom perhaps genuinely believed that the Sardar Sarovar was 'Gujarat's life-line'. It was a telling confrontation. Middle Class Urban India versus a Rural, predominantly Tribal, Army. The marching people demanded they be allowed to cross the border and walk to the dam site. The police refused them passage. To stress their commitment to non-violence, each villager had his or her hands bound together. One by one, they defied the battalions of police. They were beaten, arrested and dragged into waiting trucks in which they were driven off and dumped some miles away, in the wilderness. They just walked back and began all over again.

The face-off continued for almost two weeks. Finally, on 7th January 1991, the seven members of the sacrificial squad announced that they were going on an indefinite hunger strike. Tension rose to dangerous levels. The Indian and international Press, TV camera crews and documentary filmmakers, were present in force. Reports appeared in the papers almost every day. Environmental Activists stepped up the pressure in Washington. Eventually, acutely embarrassed by the glare of unfavourable media, the World Bank announced that it would commission an Independent Review of the Sardar Sarovar

Projects - unprecedented in the history of Bank Behaviour.
When the news reached the valley, it was received with distrust
and uncertainty. The people had no reason to trust the World
Bank. But still, it was a victory of sorts. The villagers,
understandably upset by the frightening deterioration in the
condition of their comrades who had not eaten for 22 days,
pleaded with them to call off the fast. On 28th January, the fast at
Ferkuwa was called off and the brave, ragged army returned to
their homes shouting *"Hamara Gaon Mein Hamara Raj!"* (Our
Rule in Our Villages).

There has been no army quite like this one, anywhere else in
the world. In other countries - China (Chairman Mao got a Big
Dam for his 77th birthday), Malaysia, Guatemala, Paraguay - every
sign of revolt has been snuffed out almost before it began. Here
in India, it goes on and on. Of course, the State would like to
take credit for this too. It would like us to be grateful to it for
not crushing the movement completely, for *allowing* it to exist.
After all what *is* all this, if not a sign of a healthy functioning
democracy in which the State has to intervene when its people
have differences of opinion?
I suppose that's one way of looking at it. (Is this my cue to
cringe and say "Thankyou, thankyou, for allowing me to write
the things I write?")
We don't need to be grateful to the State for permitting us to
protest. We can thank ourselves for that. It is we who have
insisted on these rights. It is we who have refused to surrender
them. If we have anything to be truly proud of as a people, it is
this.
The struggle in the Narmada valley lives, *despite* the State.

The Indian State makes war in devious ways. Apart from its
apparent benevolence, its other big weapon is its ability to wait.
To roll with the punches. To wear out the opposition. The
State never tires, never ages, never needs a rest. It runs an endless

relay.

But fighting people tire. They fall ill, they grow old. Even the young age prematurely. For twenty years now, since the Tribunal's award, the ragged army in the valley has lived with the fear of eviction. For twenty years, in most areas there has been no sign of 'development' - no roads, no schools, no wells, no medical help. For twenty years, it has borne the stigma 'slated for submergence' - so it's isolated from the rest of society (no marriage proposals, no land transactions). They're a bit like the Hibakushas in Japan (the victims and their descendants of the bombing in Hiroshima and Nagasaki). The 'fruits of modern development', when they finally came, brought only horror. Roads brought surveyors. Surveyors brought trucks. Trucks brought policemen. Policemen brought bullets and beatings and rape and arrest and in one case, murder. The only genuine 'fruit' of modern development that reached them, reached them inadvertently - the right to raise their voices, the right to be heard. But they have fought for twenty years now. How much longer will they last?

The struggle in the valley is tiring. It's no longer as fashionable as it used to be. The international camera crews and the radical reporters have moved (like the World Bank) to newer pastures. The documentary films have been screened and appreciated. Everybody's sympathy is all used up. But the dam goes on. It's getting higher and higher...

Now, more than ever before, the ragged army needs reinforcements. If we let it die, if we allow the struggle to be crushed, if we allow the people to be brutalized, we will lose the most precious thing we have: our spirit, or what's left of it.

"India will go on," they'll tell you, the sage philosophers who don't want to be troubled by piddling Current Affairs. As though 'India' is somehow more valuable than her people.

Old Nazis probably soothe themselves in similar ways.
It's too late, some people say. Too much time and money has
gone into the project to revoke it now.

So far, the Sardar Sarovar reservoir has submerged only a fourth
of the area that it will when (if) the dam reaches its full height. If
we stop it now, we would save 325,000 people from certain
destitution. As for the economics of it - it's true that the
Government has already spent Rs. 7,500 crores, but continuing
with the project would mean throwing good money after bad.
We would save something like Rs.35,000 crores of public money,
enough to fund local water harvesting projects in every village
in this vast country.What could possibly be a more worthwhile
war?

The war for the Narmada Valley is not just some exotic tribal
war, or a remote rural war or even an exclusively Indian war. It's
a war for the rivers and the mountains and the forests of the
world. All sorts of warriors from all over the world, anyone who
wishes to enlist, will be honoured and welcomed. Every kind
of warrior will be needed. Doctors, lawyers, teachers, judges,
journalists, students, sportsmen, painters, actors, singers, lovers
.... The borders are open, folks! Come on in.

Anyway, back to the story.

In June 1991, the World Bank appointed Bradford Morse, a
former head of the United Nations Development Program, as

Chairman of the Independent Review. His brief was to make a thorough assessment of the Sardar Sarovar Projects. He was guaranteed free access to all secret Bank documents relating to the Projects.

Morse and his team arrived in India in September 1991. The NBA, convinced that this was yet another set-up, at first refused to meet them. The Gujarat Government welcomed the team with a red carpet (and a nod and a wink) as covert allies.

A year later, in June 1992, the historic Independent Review (known also as the Morse Report) was published.

The Independent Review unpeels the project delicately, layer by layer, like an onion. Nothing was too big, and nothing too small for the members of the Morse Committee to enquire into. They met ministers and bureaucrats, they met NGOs working in the area, went from village to village, from re-settlement site to resettlement site. They visited the good ones. The bad ones. The temporary ones, the permanent ones. They spoke to hundreds of people. They travelled extensively in the submergence area and the command area. They went to Kutch and other drought-hit areas in Gujarat. They commissioned their own studies. They examined every aspect of the project: hydrology and water management, the upstream environment, sedimentation, catchment area treatment, the downstream environment, the anticipation of likely problems in the command area - water-logging, salinity, drainage, health, the impact on wildlife.

What the Independent Review reveals, in temperate, measured tones (which I admire, but cannot achieve) is scandalous. It is the most balanced, unbiased, yet damning indictment of the relationship between the Indian State and the World Bank. Without appearing to, perhaps even without intending to, the report cuts through to the cosy core, to the space where they live together and love each other (somewhere between what they say and what they do).

The core recommendation of the 357 page Independent Review was unequivocal and wholly unexpected:

> " We think the Sardar Sarovar Projects as they stand are flawed, that resettlement and rehabilitation of all those displaced by the Projects is not possible under prevailing circumstances, and that environmental impacts of the Projects have not been properly considered or adequately addressed. Moreover we believe that the Bank shares responsibility with the borrower for the situation that has developed...it seems clear that engineering and economic imperatives have driven the Projects to the exclusion of human and environmental concerns... India and the states involved... have spent a great deal of money. No one wants to see this money wasted. But we caution that it may be more wasteful to proceed without full knowledge of the human and environmental costs... As a result, we think that the wisest course would be for the Bank to step back from the Projects and consider them afresh..."[48]

Four committed, knowledgeable, truly independent men - they do a lot to make up for the faith eroded by hundreds of other venal ones who are paid to do similar jobs.

The Bank however, was still not prepared to give up. It continued to fund the project. Two months after the Independent Review, it sent out the Pamela Cox Committee which did exactly what the Morse Review had cautioned against ("....it would be irresponsible for us to patch together a series of recommendations on implementation when the flaws in the

31

Projects are as obvious as they seem to us..."[49]) and suggested a sort of patchwork remedy to try and salvage the operation. In October 1992, on the recommendation of the Pamela Cox Committee, the Bank asked the Indian Government to meet some minimum, primary conditions within a period of six months.[50] Even that much, the Government couldn't do. Finally, on 30th March 1993, the World Bank pulled out of the Sardar Sarovar Projects. (Actually, technically, on 29th March, one day *before* the deadline, the Government of India asked the World Bank to withdraw).[51] Details. Details.

No-one has ever managed to make the World Bank step back from a project before. Least of all a rag-tag army of the poorest people in one of the world's poorest countries. A group of people whom Lewis Preston, then President of The Bank, never managed to fit into his busy schedule when he visited India.[52] Sacking The Bank was and is a huge moral victory for the people in the valley.

The euphoria didn't last. The Government of Gujarat announced that it was going to raise the $200 million shortfall on its own and push ahead with the project.

During the period of the Independent Review and after it was published, confrontation between people and the Authorities continued unabated in the valley - humiliation, arrests, lathi charges. Indefinite fasts terminated by temporary promises and permanent betrayals. People who had agreed to leave the valley and be resettled had begun returning to their villages from their resettlement sites. In Manibeli, a village in Maharashtra and one of the nerve-centres of the resistance, hundreds of villagers participated in a Monsoon Satyagraha. In 1993, families in Manibeli remained in their homes as the waters rose. They clung to wooden posts with their children in their arms and refused to move. Eventually policemen prised them loose and dragged them away. The NBA declared that if the Government did not agree to review the project, on 6th August 1993 a band of activists would drown themselves in the rising waters of the reservoir. On 5th August, the Union Government constituted yet another committee called the Five Member Group (FMG) to review the Sardar Sarovar Projects.

The Government of Gujarat refused them entry into Gujarat.[53]

The FMG report[54] (a "desk report") was submitted the following year. It tacitly endorsed the grave concerns of the Independent Review. But it made no difference. Nothing changed. This is another of the State's tested strategies. It kills you with committees.

In February 1994, the Government of Gujarat ordered the permanent closure of the sluice gates of the dam.

In May 1994, the NBA filed a writ petition in the Supreme Court questioning the whole basis of the Sardar Sarovar dam and seeking a stay on its construction.[55]

That monsoon, when the water level in the reservoir rose and smashed down on the other side of the dam, 65,000 cubic metres of concrete and 35,000 cubic metres of rock were torn out of a stilling basin, leaving a crater 65 metres wide. The riverbed powerhouse was flooded. The damage was kept secret for months.[56] Reports started appearing about it in the press only in January of 1995.

In early 1995, on the grounds that the rehabilitation of displaced people had not been adequate, the Supreme Court ordered work on the dam to be suspended until further notice.[57] The height of the dam was 80 metres above mean sea level.

Meanwhile, work had begun on two more dams in Madhya Pradesh - the Narmada Sagar (without which the Sardar Sarovar loses 17% to 30% of its efficiency[58]) and the Maheshwar dam. The Maheshwar dam is next in line, upstream from the Sardar Sarovar. The Government of Madhya Pradesh has signed a Power Purchase contract with a private company - S.Kumars - one of India's leading textile magnates.

Tension in the Sardar Sarovar area abated temporarily and the battle moved upstream, to Maheshwar, in the fertile plains of Nimad.

The case pending in the Supreme Court led to a palpable easing of repression in the valley. Construction work had stopped on the dam, but the rehabilitation charade continued. Forests (slated for submergence) continued to be cut and carted away in trucks, forcing people who depended on them for a livelihood to move out.
Even though the dam is nowhere near its eventual projected height, its impact on the environment and the people living along the river is already severe.
Around the dam site and the nearby villages, the number of cases of malaria has increased six-fold.[59]

Several kilometres upstream from the Sardar Sarovar dam, huge deposits of silt, hip-deep and over two hundred metres wide, has cut off access to the river. Women carrying water pots now have to walk miles, literally *miles*, to find a negotiable entry point. Cows and goats get stranded in it and die. The little single-log boats that tribal people use, have become unsafe on the irrational circular currents caused by the barricade downstream.

Further upstream, where the silt deposits have not yet become a problem, there's another tragedy. Landless people, (predominantly tribal people and Dalits) have traditionally cultivated rice, melons, cucumbers and gourds on the rich, shallow silt banks the river leaves when it recedes in the dry

34

months. Every now and then, the engineers manning the Bargi dam (way upstream, near Jabalpur) release water from the reservoir without warning. Downstream, the water level in the river suddenly rises. Hundreds of families have had their crops washed away several times, leaving them with no livelihood.

Suddenly they can't trust their river anymore. It's like a loved one who has developed symptoms of psychosis. Anyone who has loved a river can tell you that the loss of a river is a terrible, aching thing. But I'll be rapped on the knuckles if I continue in this vein. When we're discussing the Greater Common Good there's no place for sentiment. One must stick to facts. Forgive me for letting my heart wander.

Silt deposits along the river bank

The State Governments of Madhya Pradesh and Maharashtra continue to be completely cavalier in their dealings with displaced people. The Government of Gujarat has a rehabilitation policy (on paper) that makes the other two states look medieval. It boasts of being the best rehabilitation package in the world.[60] It offers land for land to displaced people from Maharashtra and Madhya Pradesh and recognises the claims of 'encroachers' (usually tribal people with no papers). The deception however, lies in its definition of who qualifies as 'Project Affected.'

In point of fact, the Government of Gujarat hasn't even managed to rehabilitate people from its own 19 villages slated for submergence, let alone the rest of the 226 villages in the other two states. The inhabitants of these19 villages have been scattered to 175 separate rehabilitation sites. Social links have been smashed, communities broken up.

In practice, the resettlement story (with a few 'Ideal Village' exceptions) continues to be one of callousness and broken promises. Some people have been given land, others haven't. Some have land that is stony and uncultivable. Some have land that is irredeemably water-logged. Some have been driven out by landowners who had sold their land to the Government but hadn't been paid.[61]

Some who were resettled on the periphery of other villages have been robbed, beaten and chased away by their host villagers. There have been instances when displaced people from two different dam projects have been allotted contiguous lands. In one case, displaced people from *three* dams - the Ukai dam, the Sardar Sarovar dam and the Karjan dam - were resettled in the *same* area.[62] In addition to fighting amongst themselves for resources - water, grazing land, jobs - they had to fight a group of landless labourers who had been sharecropping the land for absentee landlords who had subsequently sold it to the Government.

There's another category of displaced people - people whose lands have been acquired by the Government for Resettlement Sites. There's a pecking order even amongst the wretched - Sardar Sarovar 'oustees' are more glamorous than other 'oustees' because they're occasionally in the news and have a case in court. (In other Development Projects where there's no press, no NBA, no court case, there are no records. The displaced leave no trail at all.)

In several resettlement sites, people have been dumped in rows of corrugated tin sheds which are furnaces in summer and 'fridges in winter. Some of them are located in dry river beds which, during the monsoon, turn into fast-flowing drifts. I've been to some of these 'sites'. I've seen film footage[63] of others: shivering children, perched like birds on the edges of charpais, while swirling waters enter their tin homes. Frightened, fevered eyes watch pots and pans carried through the doorway by the current, floating out into the flooded fields, thin fathers swimming after them to retrieve what they can.

When the waters recede they leave ruin. Malaria, diahorrea, sick cattle stranded in the slush. The ancient teak beams dismantled from their previous homes, carefully stacked away like postponed dreams, now spongy, rotten and unusable.

Tin shed rehabilitation sites. They are called "transit huts", suggesting that they are only temporary, but people have been living in them for over seven years.

Forty households were moved from Manibeli to a resettlement site in Maharashtra. In the first year, thirty-eight children died.[64] In today's papers (Indian Express, 26th April '99) there's a report about nine deaths in a single rehabilitation site in Gujarat. In the course of a single week. That's 1.2875 PAPs a day, if you're counting.

Many of those who have been resettled are people who have lived all their lives deep in the forest with virtually no contact with money and the modern world. Suddenly they find themselves left with the option of starving to death or walking several kilometres to the nearest town, sitting in the marketplace (both men and women) offering themselves as wage labour, like goods on sale.

Instead of a forest from which they gathered everything they needed - food, fuel, fodder, rope, gum, tobacco, tooth powder, medicinal herbs, housing materials - they earn between ten and twenty rupees a day with which to feed and keep their families. Instead of a river, they have a hand pump. In their old villages, they had no money, but they were insured. If the rains failed, they had the forests to turn to. The river to fish in. Their livestock was their fixed deposit. Without all this, they're a heartbeat away from destitution.

In Vadaj, a resettlement site I visited near Baroda, the man who was talking to me rocked his sick baby in his arms, clumps of flies gathered on its sleeping eyelids. Children collected around us, taking care not to burn their bare skin on the scorching tin walls of the shed they call a home. The man's mind was far away from the troubles of his sick baby. He was making me a list of the fruit he used to pick in the forest. He counted forty-eight kinds. He told me that he didn't think he or his children would ever be able to afford to eat any fruit again. Not unless he stole it. I asked him what was wrong with his baby. He said it would

38

be better for the baby to die than live like this. I asked what the baby's mother thought about that. She didn't reply. She just stared.

For the people who've been resettled, everything has to be re-learned. Every little thing, every big thing: from shitting and pissing (where d'you do it when there's no jungle to hide you?) to buying a bus ticket, to learning a new language, to understanding money. And worst of all, learning to be supplicants. Learning to take orders. Learning to have Masters. Learning to answer only when you're addressed.
In addition to all this, they have to learn how to make written representations (in triplicate) to the Grievance Redressal Committee or the Sardar Sarovar Narmada Nigam for any particular problems they might have. Recently, 3,000 people came to Delhi to protest their situation - travelling overnight by train, living on the blazing streets.[65] The President wouldn't meet them because he had an eye infection. Maneka Gandhi, the Minister for Social Justice and Empowerment, wouldn't meet them but asked for a written representation *(Dear Maneka, Please don't build the dam, Love, The People)*. When the representation was handed to her she scolded the little delegation for not having written it in English.

From being self-sufficient and free, to being impoverished and yoked to the whims of a world you know nothing, *nothing* about - what d'you suppose it must feel like? Would you like to trade your beach house in Goa for a hovel in Paharganj? No? Not even for the sake of the Nation?

Truly, it is just not possible for a State Administration, *any* State Administration, to carry out the rehabilitation of a people as fragile as this, on such an immense scale. It's like using a pair of hedge-shears to trim an infant's finger nails. You can't do it without shearing its fingers off.

39

Land for land sounds like a reasonable swap, but how do you implement it? How do you uproot 200,000 people (the official blinkered estimate) - of which 117,000 are tribal people - and relocate them in a humane fashion? How do you keep their communities intact in a country where every inch of land is fought over, where almost all litigation pending in courts has to do with land disputes?
Where is all this fine, unoccupied but arable land that is waiting to receive these intact communities?

The simple answer is that there isn't any. Not even for the 'officially' displaced of this one dam.

What about the rest of the 3,299 dams?
What about the remaining thousands of 'PAPs' earmarked for annihilation? Shall we just put the Star of David on their doors and get it over with?

The reservoir of the Maheshwar dam will wholly or partially submerge 60 villages in the Nimad plains of Madhya Pradesh. A significant section of the population in these villages - roughly a third - are Kevats and Kahars, ancient communities of ferrymen, fisherfolk, sand quarriers and cultivators of drawdown silt banks. Most of them own no land, but the river sustains them, and means more to them than to any one else. When the dam is built, thousands of Kevats and Kahars will lose their only source of livelihood. Yet, simply because they are landless, they do not qualify as Project-affected and will not be eligible for rehabilitation.

Jalud is the first of sixty villages that will be submerged by the reservoir of the Maheshwar dam. Jalud is not a tribal village, and is therefore riven with the shameful caste divisions that are the scourge of every ordinary Hindu village. A majority of the land owning farmers (the ones who qualify as PAPs) are Rajputs. They farm some of the most fertile soil in India. Their houses are piled with sacks of wheat and daal and rice. They boast so much about the things they grow on their land that if it weren't so tragic, it could get on your nerves. Their houses have already begun to crack with the impact of the dynamiting on the dam site.

Protesting against the Maheshwar dam.

Twelve families who had small holdings in the vicinity of the dam site had their land acquired. They told me how when they objected, cement was poured into their water pipes, their standing crops were bulldozed and the police occupied the land by force. All twelve families are now landless and work as wage labour.

The area that the Rajputs of Jalud are going to be moved to is a few kilometres inland, away from the river, adjoining a predominantly Dalit and tribal precinct in a village called Samraj. I saw the huge tract of land that had been marked off for them. It was a hard, stony hillock with stubbly grass and scrub, on which truckloads of silt were being unloaded and spread out in a thin layer to make it look like rich, black cotton soil.

The story goes like this: on behalf of the the S.Kumars (Textile Tycoons turned Nation Builders) the District Magistrate acquired the hillock, which was actually village common grazing land that belonged to the people of Samraj. In addition to this, the land of 34 Dalit and tribal villagers was acquired. No compensation was paid.

The villagers, whose main source of income was their livestock, had to sell their goats and buffaloes because they no longer had anywhere to graze them. Their only remaining source of income lies (lay) on the banks of a small lake on the edge of the village. In summer, when the water level recedes, it leaves a shallow ring of rich silt on which the villagers grow (grew) rice and melons and cucumber.
The S.Kumars have excavated this silt, to cosmetically cover the stony grazing ground (that the Rajputs of Jalud don't want). The banks of the lake are now steep and uncultivable.
The already impoverished people of Samraj have been left to starve, while this photo opportunity is being readied for German and Swiss funders, Indian courts and anybody else who cares to pass that way.

This is how India works. This is the genesis of the Maheshwar dam. The story of the first village. What will happen to the other fifty-nine? May bad luck pursue this dam. May bulldozers turn upon the Textile Tycoons.
Nothing can justify this kind of behaviour.

In circumstances like these, to even entertain a debate about Rehabilitation is to take the first step towards setting aside the Principles of Justice. Resettling 200,000 people in order to take (or pretend to take) drinking water to 40 million - there's something very wrong with the *scale* of operations here. This is

Fascist Maths. It strangles stories. Bludgeons detail. And manages to blind perfectly reasonable people with its spurious, shining vision.

When I arrived on the banks of the Narmada in late March 1999, it was a month after the Supreme Court had suddenly vacated the stay on construction work of the Sardar Sarovar dam. I had read pretty much everything I could lay my hands on (all those 'secret' Government documents). I had a clear idea of the lay of the land - of what had happened where and when and to whom. The story played itself out before my eyes like a tragic film whose actors I'd already met. Had I not known its history, nothing would have made sense. Because in the valley there are stories within stories and it's easy to lose the clarity of rage in the sludge of other peoples' sorrow.

I ended my journey in Kevadia Colony, where it all began.

Thirty-eight years ago, this is where the Government of Gujarat decided to locate the infrastructure it would need for starting work on the dam: guest houses, office blocks, accommodation for engineers and their staff, roads leading to the dam site, warehouses for construction material.

It is located on the cusp of what is now the Sardar Sarovar reservoir and the Wonder Canal, Gujarat's 'lifeline', that is going to quench the thirst of millions.

Nobody knows this, but Kevadia Colony is the key to the World. Go there, and secrets will be revealed to you.

In the winter of 1961, a government officer arrived in a village called Kothie and told the villagers that some of their land would be needed to construct a helipad because someone terribly important was going to come visiting. In a few days, a bulldozer arrived and flattened standing crops. The villagers were made to sign papers and were paid a sum of money, which they assumed was payment for their destroyed crops. When the helipad was ready, a helicopter landed on it, and out came Prime Minister Nehru. Most of the villagers couldn't see him because he was surrounded by policemen. Nehru made a speech. Then he pressed a button and there was an explosion on the other side of the river. After the explosion he flew away.[66] That was the genesis of what was to become the Sardar Sarovar dam.

Could Nehru have known when he pressed that button that he had unleashed an incubus?

After Nehru left, the Government of Gujarat arrived in strength. It acquired 1,600 acres of land from 950 families from six villages.[67] The people were Tadvi tribals who, because of their proximity to the city of Baroda, were not entirely unversed in the ways of a market economy. They were sent notices and told that they would be paid cash compensations and given jobs on the dam site. Then the nightmare began.

Trucks and bulldozers rolled in. Forests were felled, standing crops destroyed. Everything turned into a whirl of jeeps and engineers and cement and steel. Mohan Bhai Tadvi watched eight acres of his land with standing crops of jowar, toovar and cotton being levelled. Overnight he became a landless labourer. *Three years later* he received his cash compensation of Rs. 250 an acre in three separate instalments.

Dersukh Bhai Vesa Bhai's father was given Rs. 3,500 for his house and five acres of land with its standing crops and all the trees on it. He remembers walking all the way to Rajpipla (the district headquarters) as a little boy, holding his father's hand.

He remembers how terrified they were when they were called in to the Tehsildar's office. They were made to surrender their compensation notices and sign a receipt. They were illiterate, so they didn't know how much the receipt was made out for.

Everybody had to go to Rajpipla but they were always summoned on different days, one by one. So they couldn't exchange information or compare stories.

Gradually, out of the dust and bulldozers, an offensive, diffuse configuration emerged. Kevadia Colony. Row upon row of ugly cement flats, offices, guest houses, roads. All the graceless infrastructure of Big Dam construction. The villagers' houses were dismantled and moved to the periphery of the colony where they remain today, squatters on their own land. Those that caused trouble were intimidated by the police and the construction company. The villagers told me that in the contractor's headquarters they have a 'lock-up' like a police lock-up, where recalcitrant villagers are incarcerated and beaten.

The people who were evicted to build Kevadia Colony do not qualify as 'Project-Affected' in Gujarat's Rehabilitation package.

Some of them work as servants in the officers' bungalows and waiters in the guest house built on the land where their own houses once stood. Can there be anything more poignant?
Those who had some land left, tried to cultivate it, but the Kevadia municipality introduced a scheme in which they brought in pigs to eat uncollected refuse on the streets. The pigs stray into the villagers' fields and destroy their crops.

In 1992, thirty years later, each family has been offered a sum of Rs. 12,000 per acre, upto a maximum of Rs. 36,000, *provided* they agree to leave their homes and go away! Yet 40% of the land that was acquired is lying unused. The government refuses to return it. 11 acres acquired from Deviben who is a widow now, has been given over to the Swami Narayan Trust (a big religious sect). On a small portion of it, the Trust runs a little school. The rest it cultivates, while Deviben watches through the barbed wire fence. On 200 acres acquired in the village of Gora, villagers were evicted and blocks of flats were built. They lay empty for years. Eventually the Government hired it for a nominal fee to Jai Prakash Associates, the dam contractors, who, the villagers say, sublet it privately Rs. 32,000 a month. (Jai Prakash Associates, the biggest dam contractors in the country, the *real* nation-builders, own the Siddharth Continental and the Vasant Continental Hotels in Delhi.)

Kevadia Colony - Squatters on their own land. The original owners of the land sleep in the open. In the background is a derelict hostel for dam employees.

On an area of about 30 acres there is an absurd cement PWD replica of the ancient Shoolpaneshwar temple that was submerged in the reservoir. The same political formation that plunged a whole nation into a bloody, medieval nightmare because it insisted on destroying an old mosque to dig up a non-existent temple, thinks nothing of submerging a hallowed pilgrimage route and hundreds of temples that have been

46

worshipped in for centuries.

It thinks nothing of destroying the sacred hills and groves, the places of worship, the ancient homes of the gods and demons of tribal people.

It thinks nothing of submerging a valley that has yielded fossils, microliths and rock paintings, the only valley in India, according to archaeologists, that contains an uninterrupted record of human occupation from the Old Stone Age.

What can one say?

The submerged Shoolpaneshwar temple is being replaced with a cement replica built by the PWD.

In Kevadia Colony, the most barbaric joke of all is the wildlife museum. The Shoolpaneshwar Sanctuary Interpretation Centre gives you quick, comprehensive evidence of the Government's sincere commitment to Conservation.

The Sardar Sarovar reservoir, when the dam reaches its full height, is going to submerge about 13,000 hectares of prime forest land. (In anticipation of submergence, the forest began to be felled many greedy years ago). Between the Narmada Sagar dam and the Sardar Sarovar dam, 50,000 hectares of old growth broadleaved forest will be submerged. Madhya Pradesh has the highest rate of forest cover loss in the whole of India. This is partly responsible for the reduced flow in the Narmada and the increase in siltation. Have engineers made the connection between forest, rivers and rain? Unlikely. It isn't part of their brief. Environmentalists and conservationists were quite rightly alarmed at the extent of loss of biodiversity and wildlife habitat that the submergence would cause. To mitigate this loss, the Government decided to expand the Shoolpaneshwar Wildlife Sanctuary near the dam, south of the river. There is a hare-brained scheme that envisages drowning animals from the submerged forests swimming their way to 'wild-life corridors' that will be created for them, and setting up home in the New! Improved! Shoolpaneshwar Sanctuary.

Presumably wildlife and biodiversity can be protected and maintained only if human activity is restricted and traditional rights to use forest resources curtailed. 40,000 tribal people from 101 villages within the boundaries of the Shoolpaneshwar Sanctuary depend on the forest for a livelihood. They will be 'persuaded' to leave.

They are not included in the definition of 'Project Affected'. Where will they go? I imagine you know by now.

Whatever their troubles in the real world, in the Shoolpaneshwar Sanctuary Interpretation Centre (where an old stuffed leopard and a mouldy sloth bear have to make do with a shared corner) the tribal people have a whole room to themselves. On the walls there are clumsy wooden carvings, Government approved tribal art, with signs that say 'Tribal Art'. In the centre, there is a life-sized thatched hut with the door open. The pot's on the

fire, the dog is asleep on the floor and all's well with the world. Outside, to welcome you, are Mr. and Mrs.Tribal. A lumpy, papier mache couple, smiling.
Smiling. They're not even permitted the grace of rage. That's what I can't get over.

Oh, but have I got it wrong? What if they're smiling with National Pride? Brimming with the joy of having sacrificed their lives to bring drinking water to thirsty millions in Gujarat?

For twenty years now, the people of Gujarat have waited for the water they believe the Wonder Canal will bring them. For years the Government of Gujarat has invested 85% of the State's irrigation budget into the Sardar Sarovar Projects. Every smaller, quicker, local, more feasible scheme has been set aside for the sake of this. Election after election has been contested and won on the 'water ticket'. Everyone's hopes are pinned to the Wonder Canal. Will she fulfil Gujarat's dreams?

From the Sardar Sarovar dam, the Narmada flows through 180 kilometres of rich lowland into the Arabian sea in Bharuch. What the Wonder Canal does, more or less, is to re-route most of the river, bending it almost 90 degrees northward. It's a pretty drastic thing to do to a river. The Narmada estuary in Bharuch is one of the last known breeding place of the Hilsa, probably the hottest contender for India's favourite fish.

The Stanley dam wiped out Hilsa from the Cauvery River in south India, and Pakistan's Ghulam Mohammed dam destroyed its spawning area on the Indus. Hilsa, like the salmon, is an anadromous fish - born in freshwater, migrating to the ocean as a smolt and returning to the river to spawn. The drastic reduction in water flow, the change in the chemistry of the water because of all the sediment trapped *behind* the dam, will radically alter the ecology of the estuary and modify the delicate balance of fresh water and sea water which is bound to affect the spawning. At present, the Narmada estuary produces 13,000 tonnes of Hilsa and freshwater prawn (which also breeds in brackish water). 10,000 fisher families depend on it for a living.[68]

The Morse Committee was appalled to discover that no studies had been done of the downstream environment[69] - no documentation of the riverine ecosystem, its seasonal changes, biological species or the pattern of how its resources are used. The dam-builders had no idea what the impact of the dam would be on the people and the environment downstream, let alone any ideas on what steps to take to mitigate it.

The government simply says that it will alleviate the loss of Hilsa fisheries by stocking the reservoir with hatchery-bred fish. (Who'll control the reservoir? Who'll grant the commercial fishing to its favourite paying customers?) The only hitch is that so far, scientists have not managed to breed Hilsa artificially. The rearing of Hilsa depends on getting spawn from wild adults, which will in all likelihood be eliminated by the dam. Dams have either eliminated or endangered one fifth of the world's fresh water fish.[70]
So! Quiz question - where will the 40,000 fisher folk go?
E.mail your answers to the Government that Cares dot com.

At the risk of losing readers - I've been warned several times, "How can you write about *irrigation?* Who the *hell* is interested?"

- let me tell you what the Wonder Canal is and what she's meant to achieve. *Be* interested, if you want to snatch your future back from the sweaty palms of the Iron Triangle.

Most rivers in India are monsoon-fed. 80-85% of the flow takes place during the rainy months - usually between June and September. The purpose of a dam, an irrigation dam, is to store monsoon water in its reservoir and then use it judiciously for the rest of the year, distributing it across dry land through a system of canals. The area of land irrigated by the canal network is called the 'command area'.

How will the command area, accustomed only to seasonal irrigation, its entire ecology designed for that single pulse of monsoon rain, react to being irrigated the whole year round? Perennial irrigation does to soil roughly what anabolic steroids do to the human body. Steroids can turn an ordinary athlete into an Olympic medal-winner; perennial irrigation can convert soil which produced only a single crop a year, into soil that yields *several* crops a year. Lands on which farmers traditionally grew crops that don't need a great deal of water (maize, millet, barley, and a whole range of pulses) suddenly yield water-guzzling cash crops - cotton, rice, soya bean, and the biggest guzzler of all (like those finned 'fifties cars), sugar-cane. This completely alters traditional crop patterns in the command area. People stop growing things that they can afford to *eat*, and start growing things that they can only afford to *sell*. By linking themselves to the 'market' they lose control over their lives.

Ecologically too this is a poisonous payoff. Even if the markets hold out, the soil doesn't. Over time it becomes too poor to support the extra demands made on it. Gradually, in the way a steroid-using athlete becomes an invalid, the soil becomes depleted and degraded, and agricultural yields begin to decrease.[71]

In India, land irrigated by well water is today almost twice as productive as land irrigated by canals.[72] Certain kinds of soil are less suitable for perennial irrigation than others. Perennial canal irrigation raises the level of the water-table. As the water moves up through the soil, it absorbs salts. Saline water is drawn to the surface by capillary action, and the land becomes water-logged. The 'logged' water (to coin a phrase) is then breathed into the atmosphere by plants, causing an even greater concentration of salts in the soil. When the concentration of salts in the soil reaches one percent, that soil becomes toxic to plant life. This is what's called salinization.

A study[73] by the Centre for Resource and Environmental Studies at the Australian National University says that one fifth of the world's irrigated land is salt-affected.
By the mid 80's, 25 million of the 37 million hectares under irrigation in Pakistan was estimated to be either salinized or water-logged or both.[74] In India the estimates vary between 6 and 10 million hectares.[75] According to 'secret' government studies[76], more than 52% of the Sardar Sarovar Command area is prone to water-logging and salinization.

And that's not the end of the bad news.

The 460 kilometre long, concrete-lined Sardar Sarovar Wonder Canal and its 75,000 kilometre network of branch canals and sub-branch canals is designed to irrigate a total of two million hectares of land spread over 12 districts. The districts of Kutch and Saurashtra (the billboards of Gujarat's Thirst campaign) are at the very tail end of this network.

The system of canals superimposes an arbitrary concrete grid on the existing pattern of natural drainage in the command area. It's a little like reorganising the pattern of reticulate veins on the surface of a leaf. When a canal cuts across the path of a natural drain, it blocks the flow of the natural, seasonal water and leads to water-logging. The engineering solution to this is to map the pattern of natural drainage in the area and replace it with an alternate, artificial drainage system that is built in conjunction with the canals. The problem, as you can imagine, is that doing this is enormously expensive. The cost of drainage is not included as part of the Sardar Sarovar Projects. It usually isn't, in most irrigation projects.

David Hopper, the World Bank's vice-president for South Asia, has admitted[77] that The Bank does not usually include the cost of drainage in its irrigation projects in South Asia because irrigation projects *with* adequate drainage are just too expensive. *It costs five times as much to provide adequate drainage as it does to irrigate the same amount of land.* It makes the cost of a complete Project appear unviable.

The Bank's solution to the problem is to put in the irrigation system and wait - for salinity and water-logging to set in. When all the money's spent and the land is devastated and the people are in despair, who should pop by? Why, the friendly neighbourhood Banker! And what's that bulge in his pocket? Could it be a loan for a Drainage Project?

In Pakistan the World Bank financed the Tarbela (1977) and Mangla dam (1967) Projects on the Indus. The command areas are water-logged.[78] Now The Bank has given Pakistan a $785 million loan for a drainage project. In India, in Punjab and Haryana it's doing the same.

Irrigation without drainage is like having a system of arteries and no veins. Pretty damn pointless.

Since the World Bank stepped back from the Sardar Sarovar Projects, it's a little unclear where the money for the drainage is going to come from. This hasn't deterred the Government from going ahead with the Canal work. The result is that even before the dam is ready, before the Wonder Canal has been commissioned, before a single drop of irrigation water has been delivered, water-logging has set in. Among the worst affected areas are the resettlement colonies.

There is a difference between the planners of the Sardar Sarovar irrigation scheme and the planners of previous projects. At least they acknowledge that water-logging and salinization are *real* problems and need to be addressed.
Their solutions however, are corny enough to send a Hoolock Gibbon to a hooting hospital.

They plan to have a series of electronic groundwater sensors placed in every 100 square kilometres of the command area. (That works out to about 1,800 ground sensors). These will be linked to a central computer that will analyse the data and send out commands to the canal heads to stop water flowing into areas that show signs of water-logging. A network of 'Only-irrigation', 'Only-drainage' and 'Irrigation-cum drainage' tube-wells will be sunk, and electronically synchronised by the central computer. The saline water will be pumped out, mixed with mathematically computed quantities of freshwater and then re-circulated into a network of surface and sub-surface drains (for which more land will be acquired.)[79]
To achieve the irrigation efficiency that they claim they'll achieve, according to a study done by Dr Rahul Ram for Kalpvriksh[80], 82% of the water that goes into the Wonder Canal network will have to be pumped out again!
They've never implemented an electronic irrigation scheme before, not even as a pilot project. It hasn't occurred to them to experiment with some already degraded land, just to see if it works. No, they'll use our money to install it over the whole of the 2 million hectares and then see if it works.
What if it doesn't? If it doesn't, it won't matter to the planners. They'll still draw the same salaries. They'll still get their pensions

54

and their gratuity and whatever else you get when you retire from a career of inflicting mayhem on a people.

How can it possibly work? It's like sending in a rocket scientist to milk a troublesome cow. How can they manage a gigantic electronic irrigation system when they can't even line the walls of the canals without having them collapse and cause untold damage to crops and people?
When they can't even prevent the Big Dam itself from breaking off in bits when it rains?

To quote from one of their own studies *"The design, the implementation and management of the integration of groundwater and surface water in the above circumstance is complex."* [81]
Agreed. To say the least.
Their recommendation of how to deal with the complexity:
"It will only be possible to implement such a system if all groundwater and surface water supplies are managed by a single authority." [82]

Aha!

It's beginning to make sense now. Who will own the water? The Single Authority.
Who will sell the water? The Single Authority.
Who will profit from the sales? The Single Authority.
The Single Authority has a scheme whereby it will sell water by the litre, not to individuals but to farmers' co-operatives (which don't exist just yet, but no doubt the Single Authority can create Co-operatives and force farmers to co-operate).
Computer water, unlike ordinary river water, is expensive. Only those who can afford it will get it. Gradually, small farmers will get edged out by big farmers, and the whole cycle of uprootment will begin all over again.

The Single Authority, because it owns the computer water, will also decide who will grow what. It says that farmers getting computer water will not be allowed to grow sugar-cane because they'll use up the share of the thirsty millions who live at the tail end of the canal. But the Single Authority has *already* given licenses to ten large sugar mills right near the head of the canal.[83] On an earlier occasion, the Single Authority had said that only 30% of the command area of the Ukai Dam would be used for sugar-cane.[84] But sugar-cane grows on 75% of it (and 30% is water-logged).[85]

In Maharashtra, thanks to a different branch of the Single Authority, the politically powerful sugar lobby that occupies one tenth of the state's irrigated land uses *half* the state's irrigation water.

In addition to the sugar growers, the Single Authority has recently announced a scheme[86] that envisages a series of five-star hotels, golf courses and water parks that will come up along the Wonder Canal. What earthly reason could possibly justify this?
The Single Authority says it's the only way to raise money to complete the project!

I really worry about those millions of good people in Kutch and Saurashtra.

Will the water *ever* reach them?
First of all, we know that there's a lot less water in the river than the Single Authority claims there is.

Second of all, in the absence of the Narmada Sagar dam, the irrigation benefits of the Sardar Sarovar drop by a further 17 to 30%.

Third of all, the irrigation efficiency of the Wonder Canal (the

actual amount of water delivered by the system) has been arbitrarily fixed at 60%. The *highest* irrigation efficiency in India, taking into account system leaks and surface evaporation, is 35%.[87] This means it's likely that only *half* of the Command Area will be irrigated.
Which half? The first half.

Fourth, to get to Kutch and Saurashtra, the Wonder Canal has to negotiate its way past the ten sugar mills, the golf courses, the five-star hotels, the water parks and the cash-crop growing, politically powerful, Patel-rich districts of Baroda, Kheda, Ahmedabad, Gandhinagar and Mehsana. (Already, in complete contravention of its own directives, the Single Authority has allotted the city of Baroda a sizeable quantity of water.[88] When Baroda gets, can Ahmedabad be left behind? The political clout of powerful urban centres in Gujarat will ensure that they secure their share.)

Fifth, even in the (one hundred percent) unlikely event that water gets there, it has to be piped and distributed to those eight thousand waiting villages.
It's worth knowing that of the one billion people in the world who have no access to safe drinking water, 855 million live in rural areas.[89] This is because the cost of installing an energy intensive network of thousands of kilometres of pipelines, aqueducts, pumps and treatment plants that would be needed to provide drinking water to scattered rural populations is prohibitive. *Nobody* builds Big Dams to provide drinking water to rural people. Nobody can *afford* to.

When the Morse Committee first arrived in Gujarat it was impressed by the Gujarat Government's commitment to taking drinking water to such distant, rural districts.[90] The members of the Committee asked to see the detailed drinking water plans. There weren't any. (There still aren't any).

They asked if any costs had been worked out. "A few thousand crores," was the breezy answer.[91] A billion dollars is an expert's calculated guess. It's not included as part of the project cost. So where is the money going to come from?

Never mind. Jus' askin'.

It's interesting that the Farakka Barrage that diverts water from the Ganga to Calcutta Port has reduced the drinking water availability for 40 million people who live downstream in Bangladesh.[92]
At times there's something so precise and mathematically chilling about nationalism.
Build a dam to take water *away* from 40 million people. Build a dam to pretend to *bring* water to 40 million people.
Who are these gods that govern us? Is there no limit to their powers?

The last person I met in the valley was Bhaiji Bhai. He is a Tadvi tribal from Undava, one of the first villages where the government began to acquire land for the Wonder Canal and its 75,000 kilometre network. Bhaiji Bhai lost seventeen of his ninteen acres to the Wonder Canal. It crashes through his land, 700 feet wide including its walkways and steep, sloping embankments, like a velodrome for giant bicyclists.

The Canal network affects more than two hundred thousand families. People have lost wells and trees, people have had their houses separated from their farms by the canal, forcing them to

58

walk two or three kilometres to the nearest bridge and then two or three kilometres back along the other side. 23,000 families, let's say 100,000 people, will be, like Bhaiji Bhai, seriously affected. They don't count as 'Project-affected' and are not entitled to rehabilitation.

Like his neighbours in Kevadia Colony. Bhaiji Bhai became a pauper overnight.

Bhaiji Bhai of Undava

Bhaiji Bhai and his people forced to smile for photographs on government calendars. Bhaiji Bhai and his people, denied the grace of rage. Bhaiji Bhai and his people, squashed like bugs by this country they're supposed to call their own.

It was late evening when I arrived at his house. We sat down on the floor and drank oversweet tea in the dying light. As he spoke, a memory stirred in me, a sense of déjà vu. I couldn't imagine why. I knew I hadn't met him before. Then I realised what it was. I didn't recognise him, but I remembered his story. I'd seen him in an old documentary film, shot more than ten years ago in the valley. He was frailer now, his beard softened with age. But his story hadn't aged. It was still young and full of passion. It broke my heart, the patience with which he told it. I

59

could tell he had told it over and over and over again, hoping, praying, that one day, one of the strangers passing through Undava would turn out to be Good Luck. Or God.

Bhaiji Bhai, Bhaiji Bhai, when will you get angry? When will you stop waiting? When will you say "That's enough!" and reach for your weapons, whatever they may be? When will you show us the whole of your resonant, terrifying, invincible strength? When will you break the faith? *Will* you break the faith? Or will you let it break you?

Bhaiji Bhai standing at the exact spot in the canal where his house once stood

To slow a beast, you break its limbs. To slow a nation, you break its people. You rob them of volition. You demonstrate your absolute command over their destiny. You make it clear that ultimately it falls to you to decide who lives, who dies, who prospers, who doesn't. To exhibit your capability you show off all that you can do, and how easily you can do it. How easily you could press a button and annihilate the earth. How you can start a war, or sue for peace. How you can snatch a river away from one and gift it to another. How you can green a desert, or fell a forest and plant one somewhere else. You use caprice to fracture a peoples' faith in ancient things - earth, forest, water, air.

Once that's done, what do they have left? Only you. They will turn to you, because you're all they have. They will love you even while they despise you. They will trust you even though they know you well. They will vote for you even as you squeeze the very breath from their bodies. They will drink what you give them to drink. They will breathe what you give them to breathe. They will live where you dump their belongings. They have to. What else can they do? There's no higher court of redress. You are their mother and their father. You are the judge and the jury. You are the World. You are God.

Power is fortified not just by what it destroys, but also by what it creates. Not just by what it takes, but also by what it gives. And Powerlessness reaffirmed not just by the helplessness of those who have lost, but also by the gratitude of those who have (or *think* they have) gained.

This cold, contemporary cast of power is couched between the lines of noble-sounding clauses in democratic-sounding constitutions. It's wielded by the elected representatives of an ostensibly free people. Yet no monarch, no despot, no dictator in any other century in the history of human civilisation has had access to weapons like these.

Day by day, river by river, forest by forest, mountain by mountain, missile by missile, bomb by bomb - almost without our knowing it - we are being broken.

Big Dams are to a Nation's 'Development' what Nuclear Bombs are to its Military Arsenal. They're both weapons of mass destruction. They're both weapons Governments use to control their own people. Both Twentieth Century emblems that mark a point in time when human intelligence has outstripped its own instinct for survival. They're both malignant indications of a civilisation turning upon itself. They represent the severing of the link, not just the link - the *understanding* - between human beings and the planet they live on. They scramble the intelligence that connects eggs to hens, milk to cows, food to forests, water to rivers, air to life and the earth to human existence.

Can we unscramble it?

Maybe. Inch by inch. Bomb by bomb. Dam by dam. Maybe by fighting specific wars in specific ways. We could begin in the Narmada valley.

This July will bring the last monsoon of the Twentieth Century. The ragged army in the Narmada Valley has declared that it will not move when the waters of the Sardar Sarovar reservoir rise to claim its lands and homes. Whether you love the dam or hate it, whether you want it or you don't, it is in the fitness of things that you understand the price that's being paid for it. That you have the courage to watch while the dues are cleared and the books are squared.

Our dues. Our books. Not theirs.

Be there.

References

[1] CVJ Sharma (ed), 1989 *Modern Temples of India: Selected Speeches of Jawaharlal Nehru at Irrigation and Power Projects*, p 40-49. Central Board of Irrigation and Power

[2] Patrick McCully, 1998 *Silenced Rivers:The Ecology and Politics of Large Dams*, p 80. Orient Longman, Hyderabad

[3] From (uncut) film footage of Bargi dam oustees, 1995, Anurag Singh and Jharana Jhaveri, Jan Madhyam, New Delhi

[4] CVJ Sharma (ed), 1989, op cit, p 52-56. In a speech given before the 29th Annual Meeting of the Central Board of Irrigation and Power (17th November 1958) Nehru said, "For some time past, however, I have been beginning to think that we are suffering from what we may call 'the disease of gigantism'. We want to show that we can build big dams and do big things. This is a dangerous outlook developing in India... the idea of big - having big undertakings and doing big things for the sake of showing that we can do big things - is not a good outlook at all." And "...It is...the small irrigation projects, the small industries and the small plants for electric power, which will change the face of the country far more than half a dozen big projects in half a dozen places."

[5] Centre for Science and Environment, 1997 *Dying Wisdom: Rise, Fall and Potential of India's Traditional Water Harvesting Systems*, p 399. CSE, New Delhi; Madhav Gadgil, Ramachandra Guha, 1995 *Ecology and Equity* p 39. Penguin India, N.Delhi

[6] Indian Water Resources Society, 1998 *Five decades of Water*

Resources Development in India, p 7

[7] World Resource Institute, 1998 *World Resources 1998-99,* p 251. OUP, Oxford, UK

[8] McCully, 1998, op cit, p 26-29. See also The Ecologist Asia, Vol. 6, No.5 (Sept.-Oct. 1998), p 50-51 for excerpts of speech by Bruce Babbit, US Interior Secretary, in August 1998.

[9] Besides McCully, 1998, op cit; see:- the CSE's *State of India's Environment,* 1999, 1985 and 1982; Nicholas Hildyard and Edward Goldsmith, 1984 *The Social and Environmental Impacts of Large Dams,* Wadebridge Ecological Centre, Cornwall, UK; Satyajit Singh, 1997 *Taming the Waters: The political Economy of Large Dams,* OUP, N.Delhi; *India: Irrigation Sector Review of the World Bank* (1991); *Large Dams:Learning from the past, Looking to the Future,* 1997 IUCN, et al

[10] Mihir Shah & Ors, 1998 *India's Drylands: Tribal Societies and Development through Environmental Regeneration* p 51-103. OUP, N.Delhi

[11] Ann Danaiya Usher, 1997 *Dams as Aid: A Political Anatomy of Nordic Development Thinking.* Routledge, London and New York

[12] At current prices, Rs.2,20,000 crores, at constant 1996-97 prices

[13] GOI, 1999, *Ninth Five Year Plan 1997-2002 Vol. 2,* p 478. Planning Commission, New Delhi

[14] DK Mishra & R Rangachari, 1999 *The Embankment Trap* & *Some Disturbing Questions* p 46-48 and 62-63 respectively, Seminar 478 (June 1999); CSE, 1991 *Floods, Floodplains and Environmental myths*

[15] Mihir Shah & Ors, 1998, op cit, p 51-103

[16] Satyajit Singh, 1997, op cit, p 188-190; also, GOI figures for actual displacement

[17] At a Meeting in New Delhi on 21st January 1999 organized by the Union Ministry of Rural Areas and Employment, for discussions on the draft National Resettlement & Rehabilitation Policy and the Amendment to the draft Land Acquisition Act.

[18] Bradford Morse and Thomas Berger, 1992 *Sardar Sarovar: The report of the Independent Review*, p 62. Originally publ by Resource Futures International (RFI) Inc, Ottawa

[19] GOI, 28th and 29th *Report of the Commissioner for Scheduled Castes and Scheduled Tribes*, New Delhi, 1988-89

[20] 10th April, 1999 (front page), Indian Express, New Delhi

[21] GOI, 1999, *Ninth Five Year Plan 1997-2002* Vol. 2, p 437

[22] Siddharth Dube, 1998 *Words Like Freedom*, Harper Collins (India), N.Delhi; CMIE (Centre for Monitoring the Indian Economy), 1996. See also *World Bank Poverty Update*, quoted in Business Line 4th June, 1999

[23] National Human Rights Commission, *Report of the visit of the official team of the NHRC to the scarcity affected areas of Orissa*, Dec. 1996

[24] GOI *Award of the Narmada Water Disputes Tribunal* 1978-79

[25] GOI, *Report of the FMG-2 on SSP* 1995; Cf various affidavits of the Govt. of India and Govt. of Madhya Pradesh before the Supreme Court of India, 1994-98

[26] CWC *Monthly Observed Flows of the Narmada at Garudeshwar*, 1992, Hydrology Studies Orgnanisation, Central Water Commission, New Delhi

[27] *Written Submission on Behalf of Union of India,* February 1999, page 7, clause 1.7

[28] *Tigerlink* Vol.5 No.2, June 1999, p 28

[29] *World Bank Annual Reports 1993-98*

[30] McCully, 1998, op cit, p 274

[31] McCully, 1998, op cit, p 21. The World Bank started funding dams in China in 1984. Since then, it has lent around $3.4 billion (not adjusted for inflation) to finance 13 Big Dams that will cause the displacement of 360,000 people. The centrepiece of the World Bank's dam financing in China is the Xiaolangdi dam on the Yellow River, which will singlehandedly displace 181,000 people.

[32] McCully, 1998, op cit, p 278

[3] J.Vidal and N.Cumming-Bruce *The Curse of Pergau,* The Economist 5th March 1994; *Dam Price Jumped 81 million pounds Days After Deal,* The Guardian, London 19 January 1994; *Whitehall Must Not Escape Scot Free,* The Guardian, London, 12 February 1994; quoted in McCully, 1968 op cit, p 291

[34] McCully, 1998, op cit, p 62

[35] For example, see Sardar Sarovar Narmada Nigam Ltd, 1989, *Planning for Prosperity;* Babubhai J. Patel, 1992 *Progressing amidst Challenges;* C.C.Patel, 1991 *SSP, What it is and What it is not;* P.A.Raj, 1989, 1990 and 1991 editions, *Facts: Sardar Sarovar Project*

[36] Ibid; also Rahul Ram, 1993 *Muddy Waters: A Critical Assessment of the Benefits of the Sardar Sarovar Project,* Kalpavriksh, N. Delhi

[37] Morse, 1992, op cit, p 319. According to official ststistics (Narmada Control Authority, 1992, *Benefits to Saurashtra and Kutch Areas in Gujarat,* NCA, Indore), 948 villages in Kutch and 4,877 villages in Saurashtra are to get drinking water from the SSP. However, according to the 1981 census, there are only 887 inhabited villages in Kutch and 4,727 villages in the whole of Saurashtra. The Planners had simply hoovered up the names of villages from a map, thereby including the names of 211 deserted villages! Cited in Rahul Ram, 1993, op cit

[38] For example, the minutes of the various meetings of the Rehabilitation and Resettlement Sub Groups of the Narmada Control Authority, 1998-99. Also, Morse, 1992, op cit, p 51

[39] Rahul Ram, 1993, op cit, p 34

[40] See for example, the petition filed by the NBA in the Supreme Court, 1994

[41] SSNNL, 1989 *Planning for Prosperity,* Govt. of Gujarat

[42] S.Dharmadhikary, 1995 *Hydropower at Sardar Sarovar: Is it Necessary Justified and Affordable?* p 141 in W.F.Fisher (Ed.) *Towards Sustainable Development? Struggling Over India's Narmada River,* M.F.Sharpe, Armonk, N.York

[43] McCully, 1998, op cit, p 87

[44] McCully, 1998, op cit, p 185

[45] World Bank, 1994 *Resettlement and Development: The Bankwide Review of Projects Involving Resettlement 1986-1993*

[46] World Bank, 1994(ii) *Resettlement and Rehabilitation of India: A Status Update of Projects Involving Involuntary Resettlement*

[47] World Bank, *Resettlement and Development,* 1994, op cit

[48] Morse, 1992, op cit, Letter to the President p XII, XXIV and XXV

[49] Morse, 1992, op cit, p XXV

[50] Minimum conditions included unfinished appraisal of social and environmental impacts. For details, see Udall *The International Narmada Campaign,* McCully, 1992 *Cracks in the Dam: The World Bank in India,* Multinational Monitor, December 1992

[51] See the letter from the GOI to the World Bank, March 29, 1993; Press Release of the World Bank dated March 30, 1993, a copy of which can be found in Campaign Information Package of International Rivers Network, *Narmada Valley Development Project,* Vol. 1, Aug. 1998

[52] The date was 14th November 1992. Venue: Outside the Taj Mahal Hotel, Bombay, where Lewis Preston, President of the World Bank, was staying. See Lawyers Committee for Human Rights, April 1993, *Unacceptable Means: India's Sardar Sarovar Project and Violations of Human Rights: Oct. 1992-Feb. 1993,* p 10-12

[53] On the night of 20th March 1994, the NBA Office at Baroda was attacked by hoodlums simply because of a (baseless) rumour that one member of the Five Member Group Commmittee was sitting inside with members of the NBA. Some NBA activists were manhandled, and a large collection of NBA documents was burnt and destroyed.

[54] Ministry of Water Resources, GOI, 1994 *Report of the Five*

Member Group on Sardar Sarovar Project

[55] Writ Petition 319 of 1994 argued that the Sardar Sarovar Project violated the fundamental rights of those affected by the project, and that the project was not viable on social, environmental, technical (including seismic and hydrological), financial or on economic grounds. The Writ Petition asked for a comprehensive review of the project, pending which construction on the project should cease

[56] *Frontline*, 27th January 1995; *Sunday* 21st January 1995

[57] In January 1995, the Supreme Court took on record the statement of the Counsel for the Union of India that no further work on the Sardar Sarovar dam would be done without informing the Court in advance. On 4th May 1995, the Court allowed construction of "humps" on the dam, on the plea of the Union of India that they were required for reasons of safety. The Court, however, reiterated its order of January 1995 that no further construction will be done without the express permission of the Court

[58] *Report of the Narmada Water Disputes Tribunal With Its Decision*, Vol II 1979, p 102; cited in Morse, 1992, op cit, p 250

[59] Morse, 1992, op cit, p 323-329

[60] P.A.Raj, 1989, 1990, 1991, *Facts: Sardar Sarovar Project*, Sardar Sarovar Narmada Nigam Ltd, Gujarat

[61] Medha Patkar, 1995 *The Struggle for Participaton and Justice: A Historical Narrative* in Fisher William (ed.), "Toward Sustainable Development Struggling over India's Narmada River", M. Sharpe, Inc. p 159-178; S Parasuraman, 1997 *The Anti Dam Movement and Rehabilitation Policy* in Jean Dreze et al, *The Dam and the Nation*, OUP, p 26-65; minutes of various meetings of the R & R sub group of the Narmada Control Authority

[62] On my visit to the Valley in March 1999, I was told this by villagers at Mokhdi who had returned from their resettlement colonies

63 *Kaise Jeebo Re* Documentary film by Anurag Singh and Jharana Jhaveri, Jan Madhyam 1997; also, unedited footage in the NBA archives

64 Letter to the Independent Review from a resident of Parveta resettlement Colony, cited in Morse, 1992, op cit, p 159-160

65 *Narmada Manavadhikar Yatra*, that travelled from the Narmada Valley to Delhi via Bombay. It reached Delhi on April 7, 1999

66 Told to me by Mohanbhai Tadvi, in Kevadia Colony, March 1999

67 Morse, 1992, op cit, p 89-94; NBA interviews, March 1999

68 NBA interviews, March 1999

69 Morse, 1992, op cit, p 277-294

70 McCully, 1998, op cit, p 46-49

71 For a discussion on the subject, see the World Bank, 1991 *India Irrigation Sector Review*; A. Vaidyanathan, 1994 *Food, Agriculture and Water*, MIDS, Madras; McCully, 1998, op cit, p 182-207

72 The World Bank, 1991 *India Irrigation Sector Review* Vol. 2, p 7

73 Cited in McCully, 1998, op cit, p 187

74 Shaheen Rafi Khan, 1998 *The Kalabagh Controversy*, Sustainable Development Policy Institute, Pakistan; E.Goldsmith 1998 *'Learning to Live with Nature: The Lessons of Traditional Irrigation'* in The Ecologist Vol 6 No 5, Sept/Oct 1998

75 Mihir Shah & Ors, 1998, op cit, p 51; also in Goldsmith, 1998, op cit

76 Operations Research Group, 1981 *Critical Zones in Narmada Command – Problems and Prospects*, ORG, Baroda; ORG, 1982 *Regionalisation of Narmada Command*, ORG, Gandhinagar; World Bank, 1985 *Staff Appraisal Report, India, Narmada River Development – Gujarat, Water Delivery and Drainage Project*, Report No. 5108-IN; Core Consultants, 1982 *Main Report: Narmada Mahi Doab Drainage Study*,

commissioned by Narmada Planning Group, Govt. of Gujarat

[77] Robert Wade, 1997 *Greening the Bank: The Struggle over the Environment, 1970-1995*, p 661-662 in Devesh Kapur et al (Editors) *The World Bank: Its First Half Century*, Brookings Institution Press, Washington DC

[78] Shaheen Rafi Khan, 1998, op cit

[79] CES, 1992 *Pre-Feasibility Level Drainage Study for SSP Command Beyond River Mahi*, CES Water Resources Development and Management Consultancy Pvt. Ltd., New Delhi, for Govt. of Gujarat

[80] Rahul Ram, 1995 *The Best-laid Plans...* p 78 in Frontline, July 14th 1995

[81] Core Consultants 1982, op cit, p 66

[82] ibid

[83] For example, see GOI, 1995 *Report of the FMG*; or Rahul Ram, 1993 op cit

[84] Rahul Ram, 1993, op cit, p 28

[85] Rahul Ram, 1993, op cit, p 26

[86] Called the "Economic Regeneration Programme", formulated to generate funds for the cash strapped Sardar Sarovar Narmada Nigam Ltd. Under the Programme, land along the Main canal of the Narmada Project will be acquired and sold for tourist facilities, hotels, water parks, fun world sites, garden restaurants, etc. Cf The Times of India (Ahmedabad), 17th May 1998

[87] World Bank, 1991 *India Irrigation Sector Review*

[88] Written Submissions on behalf of the Petitioners (NBA) in the Supreme Court, Jan. 1999, p. 63; The Times of India (Ahmedabad), 23rd May 1999

[89] Ismail Serageldin, 1994 *Water Supply, Sanitation and Environmental Sustainability*, p 4, The World Bank, Washington DC

[90] Morse, 1992, op cit, p xxiii

[91] Morse, 1992, op cit, p 317-319

[92] McCully, 1998, op cit, p 167

Index

A

Ahmedabad 22, 57, 71
Andhra Pradesh 24

B

Badwani 25
Bangladesh 8, 58
Bargi Dam 23, 24, 35
Baroda 26, 38, 44, 57, 68, 70
Bharuch 16, 49
Big Dam 7, 8, 9, 10, 19, 21, 27, 45, 55, 57, 61, 66
Brazil 19

C

Canada 12
Central Government 17
Central Water Commission 7, 17, 66
China 13, 19, 20, 27, 66
Commissioner for Scheduled Castes and Tribes 11
compensation 11, 42, 44, 45

D

Dalit 10, 11, 34, 41, 42
Displacement 1, 3, 9, 10, 11, 12, 17, 22, 23, 24, 25,
31, 33, 35, 36, 37, 40

E

F

G

H

I

J